Social Marketing: Dominating Strategies for your Business with Social Media

(Facebook, Snapchat, Instagram, Twitter, LinkedIn, YouTube)

By

Michael Russel

This document is equipped towards giving careful and solid data as to the theme and issue cover. The distribution is sold with the possibility that the distributer is not required to render bookkeeping, formally allowed, or something else, qualified administrations. On the off chance that counsel is essential, legitimate or proficient, a honed individual in the calling ought to be requested.

From a Declaration of Principles which was acknowledged and endorsed similarly by a Committee of the American Bar Association and a Committee of Publishers and Associations.

Not the slightest bit is it legitimate to recreate, copy, or transmit any piece of this report in either electronic means or in printed design. Recording of this production is entirely denied and any capacity of this report is not permitted unless with composed authorization from the publisher. All rights reserved.

The data gave in this is expressed to be honest and reliable, in that any risk, as far as obliviousness or something else, by any use or mishandle of any approaches, procedures, or headings contained inside is the lone and articulate obligation of the beneficiary reader. By no means will any lawful obligation or fault be held against the publisher for

Contents

Introduction

I want to thank you and congratulate you for purchasing the book, "Social Media Marketing: Dominating Strategies for your Business with Social Media".

This book contains proven steps and strategies on how to enhance your business with different social media platforms.

The Twenty First Century is the Age of the Digital Media. In the quick paced, powerful universe of today, if you don't exist on the web, you don't have any presence on the planet whatsoever! Web-based social networking has turned out to be not just a stage to meet new individuals and interface with them but is the key if a man needs to have life full of energy, positive attitude and new ideas.

With regards to maintaining a business, these online networking systems turn out to be significantly more imperative! Furthermore, for an independent company, it could demonstrate the contrast between making a benefit and running into a misfortune! So staying aware of the most recent patterns via web-based networking media is a fundamental apparatus of showcasing that you can't stand to miss.

As a business person, you have to develop your fan following so as to develop your business. Online networking platforms are an awesome help as individuals nowadays need visual substance!

Social media is a superb and energizing world, and seeing each of the devices accessible will give you the confidence to build deals or set up an individual relationship with your clients. Also, best of all, these social media platforms are free to utilize. As an independent company you might not have the financial plan to employ an online networking supervisor or organization, yet utilizing web-based social networking doesn't need to be costly.

The sections in this book will help you pick up a firm handle on using Facebook, Snapchat, Instagram, Twitter, LinkedIn and YouTube. When you comprehend the capacity of every platform, you'll have the ability to explore them easily and usefully, and you can begin making buzz in a matter of seconds.

Chapter 1: Facebook

Facebook has turned into a worldwide wonder. You hear the informal organization being examined in regular discussion, regardless of whether it's in an office, classroom, or home. It has permitted individuals to interface with each other anyplace on the planet and is presently a crucial asset for organizations and brands as well. Facebook is a virtual and free route for organizations to advance themselves, achieve potential clients, and speak with existing customers. Once you have followers, you can utilize Facebook to publicize new items, offer rebate programs, and declare organization news. The main key to a powerful Facebook page? Draw in your fans. You need the general population who like your page to read your status updates, comment on and even share your updates to their companions. This is critical in light of the fact that the way Facebook chooses what to show clients in their news feed depends on whom they routinely collaborate with. If you want to be in it - without paying for the benefit then you should be worthy of their connection. Facebook Pages aren't for the lethargic, yet neither do you need to be a specialist, or post to your Page a billion times each week.

Setting up you business page:

Go to www.facebook.com and click on "create a page".

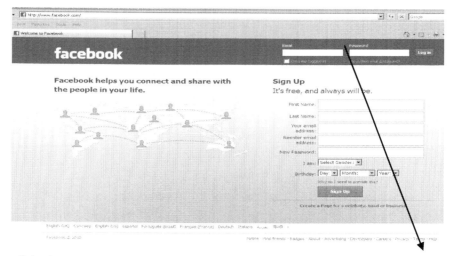

This is FREE to do and can go about as a page for your business, or just as an extra tool for marketing. You can name your page and indicate what industry your business is. To begin with choose a general category.

Now add your basic details. You will need to click to select the 'city' from a drop down list that will appear when you start typing.

When you have included these subtle elements it will inquire as to whether you have a Facebook account to connect the business page up to or you are new and need to enroll. Regardless of the possibility that you connect this up to a current account, the page won't demonstrate a connection to your own personal profile page. You will simply appear as one of the fans, and Facebook will know you to be the page admin.

Then follow the instructions given by Facebook. It will ask you to upload a profile picture for your page and a cover photo as well. Upload something which will represent your brand or product. Don't forget to add details about your page.

Posting on Facebook:

Facebook isn't like an advertisement or site that can be made and taken off alone. It's something that should be sustained, refreshed and kept alive. How frequently is regular? That is dependent upon you relying upon your time and the accessibility of new substance and thoughts. A decent dependable guideline is to attempt to refresh each couple of days – in any event once every week, however more is better. All things considered, you would prefer not to post again and again or your message will be lost in an ocean of posts.

Tips for Good Facebook Updates-

• Post photo with short details about it

• Write few sentences about something that is happening locally

• Share some good news about your business

• Display any special offers, advancements or deals (keep it brief however stuffed with info)

• Link your posts to significant blog entries or site pages

Best Business Practices on Facebook:

1. Be engaging

When creating updates for your page, you have to go for fan engagement as your principle objective.

Posting blank explanations won't get an extraordinary reaction – however, posting in a way that gets individuals' attention and rouses them to make a move pays colossal profits. You can post some questions, fill in the blanks and photos which asks questions!

2. Facebook Ads

People jump at the chance to grumble about Facebook Ads - including advertisers.

However, promotions are a key part of Facebook and they ought to be a fundamental piece of your Facebook marketing methodology.

You can't - and I rehash - CANNOT effectively grow a focused on and dynamic page without burning through cash on Facebook advertisements.

It's quite recently unrealistic nowadays.

Beyond any doubt a page goes "viral" each now and then - however smart page admins INVEST MONEY in promotions keeping in mind the end goal to discover qualified and potential clients.

We will go into more details about using Facebook Ads in our next section.

3. Being Human

Something such a large number of page owners neglect to do is be social i.e. human on their page. Your page doesn't need to be an exhausting, sterile, business-just experience. It's alright to discuss current issues. What's more, it's alright -to post in first person!

Making it Personal:

"Which post by XYZ Pizza page looks better and makes you need to lock in?"

The flavor of the day is the hawaiian personal pan pizza for $6.

or, on the other hand

Hello! Today for lunch I'm stuffing my face with this beef salami pizza! What's more, it's just $5 bucks with a glass of coke FREE! ~Garry

In addition to putting a face/name to your online presence, your page likewise needs to react like a human - not a spam robot!

Step by step instructions:

Answer to remarks utilizing the individual's initially name

Indicate Empathy

Approach individuals with Respect

Slaughter individuals with Kindness

4. Facebook Page Insights

Facebook insights and analytics are a piece of the puzzle. In any case, it's critical to venture back and see what they're truly appearing. The most essential takeaways to take from them is the thing that they enlighten admins regarding the content they're putting out.

As an entrepreneur you have to quantify the execution of your promoting endeavors - and this is where Insights offer assistance.

Fortunately, Facebook has made late enhancements that make it much less demanding to make sense of what the diverse numbers and charts mean.

5. Post Pictures

We live in a picture driven world and Facebook's the same - particularly as things move toward portable. Pictures get our consideration and are anything but difficult to expend. Beyond any doubt you can pass on something profound and significant by means of a content refresh - however then you post a senseless image and your page explodes! Photographs ought to be an essential piece of your posting methodology.

6. Contests and Prizes

People just need a chance to win stuff - end of story.

Probably the most fruitful promoting efforts done by Facebook pages are by means of contests. Facebook contests can drive colossal fan development over a brief timeframe and can have a monstrous effect to your Facebook page. If Facebook contests are run effectively with great applications and are adequately advanced, they can be to a great degree valuable for your Facebook page.

After you've got your winner, make sure to post a picture of that person and announce it on your page!

7. Pinned wall post

Research and experience reveals to us that many people will visit your page just once. They will like your page, and afterward keep on interacting with your posts that show up in their news feed – yet will infrequently (if at any time) visit your wall. Consequently, your page's essential capacity is to motivate individuals to snap that "Like" button. Facebook permits page administrators to stick one post to the highest point of their page. Make sure that the subject of this post is fascinating, extraordinary and contains an eye-catching picture.

Ad Campaigns

Facebook now offers the capacity to make advertisements and advance particular posts.

You pay for these administrations, setting a particular sum you are willing to spend on each campaign. The cost of advertisements and advancement is specifically identified with what number of fans your Page as of now has. For example, if you have around 100 fans, then your advancement could achieve three to six thousand individuals for just $5-$10. Nonetheless, when you have a large number of fans, the cost of advancement rises forcefully.

Sadly, it's anything but difficult to spend a lot of cash on your Facebook advertisements without accomplishing your coveted destinations. Advertisements can be an exceptionally compelling approach to get activity, preferences and changes, yet there are various accepted procedures (some straight from Facebook) that will diminish the expectation to absorb information and make them achieve your objectives all the more rapidly.

Targetting your audience: Advertising to an expansive, general gathering of people using no focusing on is equivalent to tossing your cash out the window. As said already, while boosting a post appropriate from your page can once in a while be powerful, setting aside the opportunity to advance a post inside your Ad Manager will as a rule help you achieve your objectives snappier.

Put your most essential content first: Users are well on the way to see content close to the start of your promotion. Hence, it's vital to put your most essential content.

Rotate advertisement every 1-2 weeks: In case you're utilizing particular focusing for your promotion (and are in this way publicizing again and again to a moderately little gathering of people), it's essential to switch up your advertisement's picture and duplicate each week or two. Utilizing a similar content again and again will bring about "advertisement weariness" or "pennant visual deficiency", diminishing the odds of your promotion getting noticed and tapped on.

Utilize a solid suggestion to take action: Always let clients recognize what you might want them to do. While you don't really should be as order as instructing them to tap on your promotion, you ought to tell them why they should click on your advertisement. This could be to exploit a deal or arrangement, to read content, to demand more data, and so on.

Put on a show with Facebook Live

Not comfortable with Facebook Live Video? Pondering what the advantages are to you and your business?

Basically:

Facebook Live let's you communicate continuously (live stream).

No more extravagant recordings.

Or, then again hours spent altering for that impeccable look and feel.

With Facebook Live, all you need to connect with your fan is the push of a button.

Additionally, the Live Video choice is incorporated ideal with Facebook. You don't have to search for a right app.

Simply open the Facebook home page of your Profile or Page, tap on the "status" button at the top, and pick the Live video symbol.

Much the same as that...

You can begin broadcasting your message and have it show up in the news feed.

Here's a couple of additional advantages:

As the video is shooting, you perceive what number of individuals are viewing the video, and in addition their names and remarks.

When it's over, the video is consequently saved to your timetable.

From that point you can share it, tweet it, install it in blog entries, or erase it.

As you can connect directly with your audience, you also have the chance to ask for their feedback. You can see their queries in the comment and reply back instantly. You can launch a new product or show the existing ones as well. Facebook live is a great way to present your products!

Responding to criticism:

Responding to comments is a vital part of your business game. You can always appreciate the positive comments but it's difficult to take in the negative reviews or comments about your brand or products.

You need to handle each negative comments with care and kindness. It's rather a challenge to take in all the negativity that comes with social media. You must respond no matter what. You have to show that you're active and that you care about their concern. Be patient and understanding while replying back to an upset fan. Put yourself in the customer's shoes and try to feel what's going on.

While you respond, ask for their advice or suggestions that will help you to improve. You can also communicate privately with any upset or angry customer.

Chapter 2: Snapchat

Why Snapchat?

Snapchat is an undeniably well known application among an extensive variety of buyers, particularly youngsters. In any case, beginning with Snapchat for your business can be somewhat scary, particularly since a large portion of the elements aren't plainly laid out.

However, if your objective clients are utilizing Snapchat, then your business ought to most likely be on it as well. Here's a well ordered manual for beginning with Snapchat.

Let's begin:

Snapchat is entirely a portable application, not a stage for the web. So agreeing to accept an account obliges you to have a cell phone. You can download Snapchat for nothing from either Google Play or App store. Once you have the application, you can agree to sign up for an account by giving your email and choosing your username and password.

Subsequent to joining, one of the principal things you'll most likely need to do is include a few contacts. On Snapchat, you can change it up of various ways. You can import the contacts from your telephone and include any individual who has Snapchat in your address book. You can likewise include individuals via looking usernames. Or, on the other hand you can take a screenshot of somebody's snap code, which is that little ghost gif that individuals can add their own photographs to. By transferring a screenshot of somebody's snap code, you can include them naturally.

Make Your Snap Code

You additionally have the chance to make your own one of a kind snap code. Simply press the huge Snapchat logo on the primary options page inside the application and you'll get the chance to take a progression of selfies. Those photographs together make up your snap code, which you can then share it to others with the goal that they can without much of a stretch add you on Snapchat.

Start posting pictures or videos

Once you've set up all your essential points of interest, it's an ideal opportunity to begin snapping. Snaps comprise for the most part of photographs or recordings. To take a photograph, you simply press the extensive round catch toward the base of the screen. Also, to take a video, you hold that button to record persistently. Snaps can be up to ten seconds in length. What's more, you can determine the measure of time you need your snaps to show up by squeezing the number at the base left of the screen.

Play with Filters

Snapchat likewise offers you the capacity to turn the camera around so you can take photographs or recordings of yourself to impart to your viewers. You may have additionally observed that many people on Snapchat utilize crazy filters that go over their appearances. There are ones that give clients puppy ears, funny voices and even limited time filters that accompany things like film release or special occasions. To get to those filters, simply press the screen all alone face and Snapchat should recognize it and raise a choice of filters that you can use for that day.

Include Some Embellishments

Regardless of the possibility that you're not attempting to utilize any bizarre voice changers or add creature ears to your snaps, there are different ways you can add some enthusiasm to your snaps after you've taken a photograph or video. Up in the upper right corner, there are buttons that enable you to include content, stickers or even doodles to your snaps. You can likewise swipe the screen to include diverse visual filters or special effects like your present speed, temperature or geo filters that demonstrate your area.

Send Your Snaps

When you're content with how your snap looks, it's an ideal opportunity to send it. There's a little arrow on the base corner of the screen that you can use to finish your snap. At that point you'll get to a page where you'll see the greater part of your contacts. You can pick which contacts you'd get a kick out of the chance to send your snap to. They'll get a notice from you and they 24 hours to view it before it vanishes.

Add to Your Story

On that same page, you'll additionally observe an option at the top that will give you a chance to send the snap to your story. Your Snapchat story resembles a collection of snaps from the day that any individual who follows you can see. This is a mainstream highlight for business Snapchat clients who need to speak with something other than a couple people at once. You can see your own particular story and perceive what number of individuals have seen it on the primary story page. You can likewise add snaps to your recollections area, which is a gathering of your most loved snaps or content that you need really saved on Snapchat.

Collaborate with Your Audience

Since you know how to set up your record and make your own particular posts, you have to consider precisely what kind of content you are going to make to get the most out of the stage. There are a lot of various ways to use Snapchat for business. The most vital thing is to remember that individuals need to utilize Snapchat to really connect with people. So consider doing things like making inquiries of your gathering of people, giving them a background look at your business, or facilitating a Q&A session. You can also share some of your most loved Snapchat accounts with others in your contact list using the new suggest feature.

Deliver private content

You can likewise utilize Snapchat to share private content that lone your supporters will get the chance to experience. Give them a first look at your new item or a sneak pinnacle of what's in store in your new accumulation. This is about being remarkable and astonishing your devotees with something extraordinary. Have a decent consider how you can convey something your adherents might not have seen some time recently.

Take your supporters on a voyage through what truly occurs in the background of your organization. This is an incredible chance to flaunt your organization and what the air resembles. You can catch recordings of staff gatherings, business trips, evening drinks or only a normal day at work. There are unlimited conceivable outcomes to show how your image is not quite the same as different brands and what your organization culture is truly similar to. It just takes one advanced mobile phone and a gathering of excited workers to make this into a Snapchat achievement.

Have you at any point pondered who the face behind online networking posts or your client benefit call is? All things considered, so have your clients. Presenting your representatives through your Snapchat story gives your devotees an individual and extraordinary knowledge into what it resembles to work at your organization. Representatives who feel esteemed and perceived will probably have a decent hard working attitude and convey energy to your organization. This positive reaction will reflect in your Snapchat story as well and it will make your devotees feel more drew in and associated with your business.

Geofilters

Snapchat's ascent has been brilliant. More than 100 million clients watch 10 billion video cuts day by day. The stage has changed video narrating, and its local instruments have extraordinary online networking showcasing esteem. Presently, you can make your own particular geofilters and utilize them to promote to your fans.

Snapchat geofilters are the ideal approach to saddle your group of onlookers' attention, since they're now processing your content. Geofilters make it less demanding for your audience to connect with and advance your item or brand naturally.

Here are some approaches to utilize Snapchat geofilters for your business.

Announcing New Product Launch

When propelling another item, you need to urge your group to discover more about it and at last make a buy. By utilizing a Snapchat geofilter, you're demonstrating your viewers that your items are essential and deserving of marked channels.

Company Culture

To advance organization culture and your business offerings, you can make a Snapchat geofilter for your office. Representatives could turn into your greatest advanced promoters as they utilize the geofilter to share to their groups. You can urge workers to share in the background occasions at your organization or meeting associates about their most loved parts of their employment.

This one-to-many sharing can affect your organization decidedly and your compass will be exponential. Sharing your organization's qualities to a bigger gathering of people will urge beat ability to need to join the group.

Promote Charity Events

Utilizing geofilters for live occasions makes a comprehensive component that connects the group. For philanthropy occasions, they can help manufacture mindfulness for a cause.

Making Snapchat geofilters for occasions will include a component of amazement and joy for your visitors and will enable individuals to share the occasion progressively. They can likewise expand perceivability and informing in a fun and viable way.

Support Your Personal Brand

Make an personal marked Snapchat geofilter in case you're going to an event or an occasion where you need to associate with similar individuals. If you have a book to offer or another collection dispatch, you can contact a radical new gathering of people.

You never know who will utilize the filters.

Image courtesy: Google

Utilize a geofilter to advance your very own image at occasions. You definitely realize that your intended interest group is there, so it's a flawless opportunity to get presentation.

Contests, Perks & Promotion

Snapchat contests are an extraordinary approach to boost individuals inside your objective market to take after and draw in with your Snapchat. Promote Snapchat contests on your other social sites as well.

The least demanding approach to run a Snapchat challenge is to request that participants send you a Snap satisfying some kind of conditions - possibly noting a question you solicit, or taking a particular type photograph or video. After the challenge due date is over, experience these Snaps -

screenshot the ones you might need to use for content later on - and select your victors either haphazardly or by picking your top picks.

Send the champs samples or codes of discount. Pick few winners to whom you'll give away items and afterward furnish different participants with codes so that they have a feeling that they've been adjusted for participating in the challenge.

Whatever you give away, ensure it's applicable to your business

Keep in mind the motivation behind building up this following is to change over them into deals later on. You need to keep participants inside your objective market as much as could be expected.

Since individuals need to follow you on Snapchat to entry and they're boosted to enter on the grounds that you'll be putting forth a prize, contests are an awesome approach to pick up devotees on Snapchat.

Sponsored contents are an awesome approach to get the message out through influencers with committed followers in your objective market.

Recognize key Snapchat influencers identified with your business with supporters who are a piece of your objective market, and contact them to accomplice up in making a supported post. This will probably cost you some cash (or no less than a product test), however it shouldn't cost as much as an Instagram or Facebook post, as Snapchat posts last a most extreme of 24 hours.

Here's some prescribed procedures for sponsored posts:

Make them look as "normal" as conceivable - send your influencer the items you'd promote so they can take pictures of, and in addition anything you'd like them to incorporate into the photograph or subtitle.

Guarantee the influencer is in the photograph, as this fortifies the brand association you're making through the supported post.

Give your influencers their own particular rebate code also. This furnishes their adherents with an extra motivating force to buy your items, and gives you an approach to track the accomplishment of your influencer showcasing effort.

Is it right for your brand?

Initially, think about your organization's shoppers clients who purchase your administrations or items. Next, think about Snapchat's client base: other than being comprising generally of youth (75% of its clients are more youthful than 25 years old starting at 2014, as indicated by Business Insider), they're likewise technically knowledgeable. They have a steady desire to take out their gadgets to record minutes, sending and communicating with information along these lines.

Not at all like Instagram and Twitter, where what you post can cost your employment, there's a lesser probability of committing errors on the fleeting stage. All in all, ask yourself, are your clients intrigued enough to escape to swing to Snapchat as one of their fundamental stages? Will probably devour news and substance from my Twitter channel, so I am not your average Snapchat client. Where does your group of onlookers assemble?

Would your organization advantage from beginning another line of correspondence? Would your shoppers mind enough that you are currently present on another stage other than Facebook and Twitter? Segments, for example, nbanking and government aren't suited for Snapchat-it is hard to pull in Snapchat's clients in case you're making content that still relates back to specific businesses (coordinations and development are two more cases of this). The innovative enterprises (like media creation) and organizations in retail can profit by Snapchat.

Chapter 3: Instagram

Instagram is an online photo/video sharing and social networking service, currently the fastest growing social platform globally since its launch in 2010. It was acquired by Facebook in 2012 and is reportedly the social network that accumulates the most engagement.

Getting Started

It goes without saying that the first thing you need to do is to download the app. It can be accessed through a web browser, but it is, first and foremost, a mobile platform, so be sure to download it on your phone! Step number two is to register your account – as a business owner, it's probably best you sign up for two accounts. Your personal account is for you and your social life, but the public account is the one you will be using to promote your company. It goes without saying that your username should be something closely related to your company's name.

When setting up your Instagram profile, it's crucial that it's both easy to find and gives a positive representation of your brand.

Firstly, you need to make sure that your username reflects your company. When signing up, make sure your company's name is in your username and in the case that you want to create multiple accounts for different branches; you may also want to include your country/region in the username too. If your brand is present on multiple social media platforms, using the same username for each account will make it easier for people to find you.

Develop a Content Strategy

Content is the establishment of your Instagram presence. Numerous organizations utilize Instagram to make their item the superstar, while many organizations frequently concentrate on organization culture and group enrollment— the correct approach is one that best grandstands your image. In light of your intended interest group and destinations, build up an arrangement to convey eye-getting substance to your group consistently.

Build up a system for breathing life into your brand's personality on Instagram, in view of your business targets. Distinguish words that mirror your image's voice and tone; the sentiments you need devotees to connect with your image; and the part you need your image to play in their lives.

Build up standard content topics, or columns, that are perfect to your image and fit the Instagram stage.

Post photographs and recordings of surprising and off camera minutes that are prompt and feel authentic. Real to life, insider access is the thing that individuals adore about Instagram.

Keep inscriptions short and new. Consolidate hashtags where important, yet not all that numerous that they bring down the effortlessness of the post.

Incorporate the area of your photograph or video when it recounts the narrative of the picture (i.e. it was taken at an occasion, roadshow, retail store, organization central command).

Incorporate video as a component of your content methodology steady with your character, voice, and substance columns.

Build Content Themes

Survey your targets and figure out what parts of your image to feature in your Instagram content. Items, administrations, colleagues and culture all offer rich potential for topic after some time. When you have a rundown of particular substance topics, conceptualize conceivable subjects for your pictures and recordings.

To set up and keep up a dynamic nearness on Instagram, decide the recurrence with which you will post. At that point you ought to build up a content date-book that goes through your topics and incorporates key dates and crusades.

A portion of the best substance for Instagram will happen suddenly, particularly if your point is to highlight organization culture or occasions. By planning content and setting a general calendar ahead of time, you can enable the adaptability to exploit openings when they happen. Amid occasions, be prepared to distribute rapidly to exploit ongoing social engagement.

If your Instagram community members are sharing their own particular content highlighting your image, you have admittance to an archive of potential content gold.

As usual, the photographs you decide to clergyman should coordinate your image tasteful. Make a point to audit clients' records and different posts before sharing their content to judge whether it is suitable to freely adjust your image to them by sharing their photograph.

You can discover client produced content on Instagram by observing your marked hashtags and business' areas.

Contests

Holding a contest on Instagram is a brilliant way of getting more Followers as well as promoting your business venture. It provides an excellent way of generating interest from prospective as well as existing customers and it also allows you to have personal, one on one interaction with them!

Choosing what you are going to give away as a prize for your contest winners is a very important decision to make, especially for a business account. You want new customers as well as repeat customers. Obviously, you will choose some part of your product to give away as the prize, but you must make sure that it's of good quality so that the winner does not feel cheated and promotes you through word of mouth, both physically as well as on social media.

#Random Selection

This is probably the simplest and the easiest way of holding a contest on Instagram. The basic premise is that you put up a post asking your Followers to like a particular photo or Follow a particular post. Give them a specific deadline within which they must do so; that is the length of the contest's validity. Once the contest is over, you will go through the list of all the people who have liked your post and then, at random, select your winner and then give them the chosen gift.

#Maximum likes contest

As the name suggests, you will choose the winner of this type of contest based on who gets the maximum likes for their pictures. What the participants have to do is simple – post a picture with a specific hashtag that you have created for this purpose or following the theme or the guideline you have set for this particular contest.

#Walk into the store contest

This is an excellent method of increasing traffic to not just your social media accounts, but your actual store as well! The rules of the contest are simple, if a bit demanding of your customers – they will have to walk into the physical store and then click pictures of themselves within the store, which they will then upload on Instagram and tag your account to it.

#Video contest

Mobile photography includes both photographs as well as videos and Instagram allows you to upload both! However, videos on Instagram have a limited length to adhere to. So keeping that in mind, a video contest is a good idea to get your customers more involved with your product. What they will have to do is post a short video, of maybe ten seconds or so, wherein they are using the product. The caption can be why they like it or what they find lacking in it – the winner can be someone of your selection or the person whose post has the most likes. It's your choice.

#Shout-out contest

This is a very simple way of getting more publicity from your followers. As you probably know, on Instagram, one way to get more followers is to do shout-outs; this basically means that when you post something, you tag another account to it and give them a shout-out, asking your followers to go and check out that person's account and if they like it, Follow them too. This kind of contest follows that premise; the winner of the contest will be the person who has given you the most number of shout-outs within the contest's specified deadline.

The 5/3/1 Strategy:

Racking up followers is no easy task. To help you doing so, you need to reach out to people. A technique that you can use to gain followers is the 5/3/1 rule:

1. Start by finding a user in your niche.

2. Like five of their photos.

3. Comment on three of their photos.

Result: Earn a new follower!

If you use hashtags correctly, users will find your posts. Exchange likes for likes, and be sure to leave a reply to commenters.

Instagram does not have a "share" feature, but apps like Report for Instagram enables you to curate users' photos.

<u>Mistakes to avoid:</u>

There's No Link in Bio to Drive Traffic

There's No Description in Your Bio

Crappy Resolution Photos Are Scaring Away Potential Customers

Your Photos Aren't Sized Right

Unpleasant Lighting is Downgrading Your Image
Where the Ever-Important Lifestyle Photos At?!

All Your Posts Look Exactly the Same

Your Content is Way Too Long and Distracting

Anticipating that Followers should Just Come to You

You're Running Contests When You Don't Have an Audience Yet

Why Are There Selfies?! It's NOT About You

Chapter 4: Twitter

Twitter is a prevalent microblogging stage where clients share short announcements including connections to pages, photographs and articles. Twitter is an extraordinary path for littler organizations to gather a fan following, declare news or promotions and react to client addresses, or even protests. Being brief in your tweeting is significant on this stage. Say what you have to state within 140 characters!

Who's on Twitter?

Entrepreneurs are regularly being encouraged to draw in on Twitter. You've heard the considerable things Twitter can accomplish for your business. How faithful fans will build your perceivability and put you miles in front of the opposition.

Yet, how genuine is it?

Some of you may think that its difficult to think considering the quantity of Twitter clients are much lower than the quantity of Facebook clients. Others may even question that social stages, for example, YouTube, Vine and Periscope would give a greater effect.

Organizations around the globe are utilizing Twitter to contact a greater target group of onlookers. Consistently,

Twitter has turned out to be a great apparatus, particularly in the deals and promoting world where income is the main thing individuals tend to see.

Twitter Terms:

• Tweet: A 140-character message.

• Retweet (RT): Re-sharing or offering credit to another person's tweet.

• Feed: The surge of tweets you see on your landing page. It's included updates from clients you take after.

• Handle: Your username.

• Mention (@): An approach to reference another client by his username in a tweet (e.g. @mashable). Clients are informed when @mentioned. It's an approach to lead exchanges with different clients in an open domain.

• Direct Message (DM): A private, 140-character message between two individuals. You can choose whether to acknowledge a Direct Message from any Twitter client, or just from clients you are taking after.

You may just DM a client who follows you.

• Hashtag (#): An approach to indicate a theme of discussion or take part in a bigger connected discourse (e.g. #AmericanIdol, #Trump). A hashtag is a disclosure device that enables others to discover your tweets, in light of themes. You can likewise tap on a hashtag to see every one of the tweets that specify it progressively — even from individuals you don't take after.

Using Hashtags

Using hashtags is a basic and essential way to deal with your posts seen by various customers. In any case, you ought to be splendid – and direct – with your hashtag utilize. How?

If you utilize Twitter for business you most likely need however many individuals as could reasonably be expected to discover it. A decent technique is to utilize hashtags that are prominent so individuals can discover your tweets when scanning for content e through this hashtag.

Hashtags are an unquestionable requirement when you compose a challenge on Twitter. Or, on the other hand should I say, when you're sorting out a well known challenge. It can be a photograph challenge or best answer challenge that require to tag a companion with the goal that battle spread as far and wide as could be allowed.

You can make your own particular hashtag with expectations that it will end up noticeably prevalent and present to you some notoriety. But if you urge clients to discuss your image, ensure you have an incredible item and administration. Else you simply entice the destiny.

You can enable yourself to be search–able to those with comparable interests and industry. You keep utilize hashtags in your profile on Twitter. Additionally incorporate a connection to your site, blog and other web-based social networking destinations.

Great advertisers have discovered accomplishment in the utilization of real–time promoting. On Twitter you can utilize real–time showcasing to watch the slanting hashtags and make it a chance to seriously add to exchanges. Thusly you can be seen by a greater group and possibly make a few connections on Twitter.

Twitter Advertising

Twitter now offers advancing options for business customers. Twitter advancing can develop your fan base and engagement – anyway it may not be as suitable as normal gathering building. It should in like manner be seen that

Twitter publicizing can be expensive.

Propelled Tweets – With this option, you pay to get your tweet before more eyes. It stays at the most noteworthy purpose of the Twitter . It's a way to deal with have your tweets gone to a greater gathering of adherents.

Propelled Trends – Want your hashtag to be a slanting point? While that can happen actually, you can pay to have your hashtag appear at the highest point of the examples list.

Propelled Accounts – Looking for more supporters? This option puts your Twitter handle into customers' "Who to Follow" box. It's fundamentally buying supporters – yet Twitter's estimations infer that you'll be appeared to customers who will presumably be enthusiastic about what you have to state.

Mistakes to avoid on Twitter:

1. Without Avatar – This is another child on the piece move that will make people doubtful of anything you say.

2. Tweeting sporadically – Regular tweeting keeps you pertinent.

3. Simply tweeting related with your site – No one appreciates a braggadocio.

4. Using an extreme number of hashtags – It looks like a spam and people won't pay attention to it.

5. No hashtags – You're feeling the loss of the opportunity to extend your range!

6. Not following anyone – Twitter is about the exchange. You should be a bit of the exchange.

7. Having a private Twitter account – If your record is private, people can't see your tweets unless you empower them to tail you. You're a business. You should require people to see and associate with you.

8. Tweeting unkind or rude contemplations – Really, no one should. Regardless, especially not from your business.

Chapter 5: LinkedIn

How to start:

We may not generally consider LinkedIn being an online networking stage, as Facebook, Twitter, and Instagram. However, it's an ideal opportunity to reconsider.

LinkedIn is essential to your business since it's a committed business network. As indicated by Statista.com, towards the finish of 2015, there were near 400 million clients on LinkedIn, all with the shared objective: to interface on a profound, proficient level.

Like whatever other online networking stage, everything begins with a profile, and despite the fact that you're hoping to develop your business' nearness, you need your very own profile in the first place.

The enormous tip for this territory is that your own profile should be an expert portrayal of yourself (your own image) and your association (your business' image).

Building you page:

Once you have your own page looking smooth, the following stride is to construct a LinkedIn Company Page.

Make your Company Page and improve it with a logo and organization subtle elements. Just like you've created your own profile, compose a depiction about your business or association and fill it with catchphrases and pertinent and intriguing data.

Outline and transfer a header or standard that speaks to your image and is predictable with your other showcasing material and online networking sites.

There's a tremendous assortment of data you can post on your Company Page, including openings for work, off camera photographs, item declarations, blog entries, new representatives, late activities, occasion audits, creator interviews... truly, the sky's the point of confinement.

But whatever you post, two fundamental standards win: it ought to convey an incentive to your group and it ought to be on brand.

Launch a LinkedIn Group:

LinkedIn Groups "give a place to experts in a similar industry or with comparative interests to share content, discover replies, post and view employments, make business contacts, and build up themselves as industry specialists.

So in what manner can your business or brand exploit LinkedIn Groups?

Join groups where your clients and prospects are - Identify bunches with individuals who are forthcoming customers or influencers in your industry and after that make substance, for example, articles, how-to's, aides and blog entries that element subjects pertinent to that gathering.

Create your group- To really manufacture group, organizations are frequently best served for a particular gathering of individuals with whom the organization plans to draw in and - significantly - who might discover an incentive in drawing in with each other, and having your organization encourage that association.

You have to be active in your group in order to establish your value and show that youself as a trusted resource. Involve other employees into discussion and always conduct your market research via polling in group.

Content Ads and Sponsored updates

LinkedIn's self-benefit stage offers two particular promotion sorts: Text advertisements and Sponsored Updates. While the two advertisement positions have some key refinements, they're both comparative in that they offer a total offer and spending control, exact focusing on and content that can drive noteworthy deals and leads for your business.

Remain unmistakable the entire day by completely subsidizing efforts as LinkedIn individuals are locked in for the duration of the day, crosswise over stages. Also, as you start to see which battles are best entertainers, move spending plan from less compelling efforts.

Don't over target or focus on an indistinguishable group of onlookers in numerous campaigns from this may make you go up against yourself in the advertisement barters. Test different messages and bits of content in each campaign to discover what reverberates best with a specific group of onlookers.

Specifically address your gathering of people inside your informing while at the same time utilizing solid visuals and nibble capable contents (ie. numbered records) to instantly snatch their attention.

Keeping in mind the end goal to make LinkedIn Sponsored Update crusades, you should first have a LinkedIn Company page. Supported Update battles can be executed in two courses: by supporting substance that you've effectively distributed to your Company page or through Direct Sponsored Content. Both are overseen through the self-serve stage, show up on desktop, versatile and tablet gadgets and inside the landing page sustain of individuals inside your intended interest group. Be that as it may, the key distinction between Sponsored Updates and Direct Sponsored Content is that the last does not show up on your Company page – consider it concealed substance just visible to individuals that are a piece of your battles' intended interest group.

Chapter 6: YouTube

Setting up your channel

1.Go to YouTube and sign in

Make a beeline for YouTube.com and snap 'sign in' in the upper right corner of the page.

At that point, sign in utilizing the Google Account you'd like your channel to be related with.

2. Go to your YouTube settings

In the upper right corner of the screen, tap on your profile symbol and after that the "Settings" gear-tooth symbol.

3. Make your channel

Under your settings, you'll see the choice to "Make a channel," tap on this connection:

Next, you'll have the choice to make an individual channel or a make a channel utilizing a business or other name. For this illustration, we'll pick the business choice.

Presently, it's an ideal opportunity to name your channel and select a classification. The channel choices accessible.

Take note of: another Google+ page will likewise be made for your image.

Congrats! You've made your YouTube channel.

Video Marketing Tips:

You can't create a viral content as you don't play piano or make videos of your pet. Rather, you ought to make content that addresses your group of onlookers' needs. Your objective should be to make recordings that are useful, important and convincing to your prospects and customers. If you can blog about it, you can make a video about it. Your video substance may comprise of how-to's, answers to regularly made inquiries, master interviews, screen video catches, slide shows and the sky is the limit from there.

Make your video findable.

Your recordings must be findable both inside and outside of YouTube. Recordings frequently show up on the primary page of web search tools, and are a demonstrated strategy for jump frogging your opposition to the highest point of the query items page. The way that Google possesses YouTube can't be disregarded.

Make a video that objectives your crowd's hunts and you'll get their consideration.

To make your video more findable, you'll need to concentrate on three key territories:

Title: Make beyond any doubt your focused on watchwords are in the initial couple of expressions of your title. Another trap is to include a colon after your underlying catchphrases and rethink your title for most extreme impact. For instance, your video on sparing cash for vacation may be called "Holiday Savings Plans: Your best solution".

Description: Two things to remember here: 1) begin your portrayal with a full URL, and 2) don't be niggardly with your portrayal—more is... well, more. Be as expressive and keyword rich as could be allowed. This will help you get discovered all the more effortlessly by individuals hunting YouTube down your sort of substance. You can likewise incorporate more URLs all through your content.

Sharing your videos:

YouTube is an online networking stage, not an island. Here are some approaches to develop the compass of your video and make it more shareable:

Blog it: Each time you post another video, you ought to make a blog entry around it. Utilize a catchphrase rich title, and fill your post with proper, corresponding content. This will convey your video to your blog endorsers and increment its odds of being found in a hunt.

Present it on Facebook.: Regardless of whether on your profile page or on your business page, you can contact a substantially more extensive group of people on Facebook. Also, video is an awesome method for expanding your popularity.

Tweet it: Great content goes more distant on Twitter.

Tips & Tricks:

Optimization: First off you need to dependably begin with the device straightforwardly accessible to you through Youtube. Presently I'm not looking at promoting, I'm all the more alluding to your titles, descriptions and keywords that are particular to your video. Do the best possible on page enhancement of your video and it will go far.

Suggestion to take action: Get individuals to like, similar to, rate and remark by utilizing call to actions (links) in your video or descriptions. You can pull individuals pretty effectively to your site with an all around set connection.

Unique content: Try not to be enticed to duplicate the accomplishment of different people without first understanding your objective specialty keeping in mind that you need to wind up being greatly disillusioned.

Be understanding and if conceivable put resources into quality recording cameras and even mouthpieces with which to record your content with. Individuals dependably cherish a channel with brilliant recordings.

Make Use of Bulletins and Subscriptions:

Explanations are utilized to highlight writings, links and other essential hotspots on your posted video. They are awesome for improving engagement with your watchers since the connections are continually driving back to your subscribe pages as well as to your official site's home page. Send notifications to your adherents each time you post something new and they will continue returning to experience some a greater amount of what you bring to the table.

Partnering Up With YouTube:

My last YouTube advertising tips and tricks to help you increment your image names' notoriety and productivity includes joining forces up with YouTube.

What happens is that each time your recordings get watched YouTube consents to pay you a specific measure of cash from the sponsors.

Conclusion

Thank you again for purchasing this book!

I hope that you have been delighted to read this book and you have found out what you have to do. I believe that you will make the rest happen. How you get it going is altogether up to you. Social media is a vast world and I'm sure that you will be able to make a fortune by using all the marketing strategies given in this book.

If you enjoyed this book, then please help us to grow by doing us a favor. Would you kindly leave a review for this book on Amazon? This will make a big difference!

Thank you and good luck!

Made in the USA
Lexington, KY
05 November 2017